Little Ones

BIG BOOK
ABOUT
SPAIN

contents page

SPANISH SQUARE, SEVILLE

IBIZA, SPAIN

SEVILLE, SPAIN

LA SAGRADA FAMILIA, BARCELONA, SPAIN

Welcome!

¡Hola! Are you ready for an unforgettable adventure in the beautiful country of Spain?

Get ready to immerse yourself in the rich culture and traditions that make Spain so unique and exciting! From the rhythmic sounds of flamenco dancing to the thrill of bullfighting, Spain has a vibrant and colourful culture that will captivate your imagination. And let's not forget about the delicious tapas, those mouth-watering small bites that are sure to delight your taste buds!

With its rich history, beautiful landscapes, and friendly people, Spain has so much to offer. So, put on your explorers' hat, grab your sunscreen, and get ready to learn all about the enchanting world of Spain. ¡Vamos! Let's go!

Take a look at a map of Europe and see if you can spot Spain! While you're exploring the map, see if you can discover other countries that surround Spain, like England and France to the north. Maps are like treasure hunts, waiting to be explored! Have fun exploring the world and discovering new places on the map!

MAP OF EUROPE

SPAIN IS LOCATED IN SOUTHWESTERN EUROPE, ON THE IBERIAN PENINSULA. IT SHARES ITS BORDERS WITH PORTUGAL TO THE WEST AND IS SURROUNDED BY THE ATLANTIC OCEAN TO THE NORTH AND WEST, THE MEDITERRANEAN SEA TO THE EAST, AND THE STRAIT OF GIBRALTAR TO THE SOUTH, WHICH SEPARATES IT FROM THE AFRICAN CONTINENT.

Flags and National Symbols

Let's learn about the flag and national symbols of Spain. Olé! The flag of Spain is called "La Rojigualda," which means "red and yellow" in Spanish. It has three horizontal stripes - two red stripes on the top and bottom, and a big yellow stripe in the middle. The red represents valor and bravery, while the yellow symbolizes generosity and peace. It's a vibrant and bold flag that proudly flies high across Spain!

But that's not all! Spain also has some fascinating national symbols. The national animal of Spain is the bull, known as "El Toro" in Spanish. Bulls are strong and powerful creatures that are admired in Spanish culture, and you might see them depicted in various forms of art and decorations. So, get ready to explore the rich culture and traditions of Spain. Vamos a descubrir España juntos! (Let's discover Spain together!) Olé!

Another important symbol of Spain is the flamenco, which is a passionate and rhythmic dance that originated in Spain. The flamenco is known for its unique music, colourful dresses, and intricate footwork, and it's a significant part of Spanish culture and identity.

Landmarks

Are you ready to explore the fascinating landmarks and monuments of Spain? Let's dive into the history and beauty of this amazing country!

Spain is filled with wonderful places, from majestic castles to ancient cathedrals and colourful palaces. One of the most iconic landmarks in Spain is the Sagrada Familia in Barcelona, a spectacular church designed by the famous architect Antoni Gaudí. There's also the Alhambra in Granada, an impressive Moorish palace and fortress with lush gardens. And we can't forget about Park Güell in Barcelona, a park filled with colorful mosaics and extravagant shapes also designed by Gaudí. These are just a few examples of the treasures you'll find in Spain. Get ready to be amazed by the unique architecture and fascinating history of these national landmarks!

The Square of Seville, also known as Plaza de España, is a grand square with a huge fountain in the center, surrounded by a crescent-shaped building adorned with beautiful ceramic tiles.

Deep in the heart of Spain, stands the mighty Templar Castle! This ancient fortress, with its towering walls and mysterious aura, has stood the test of time for centuries.

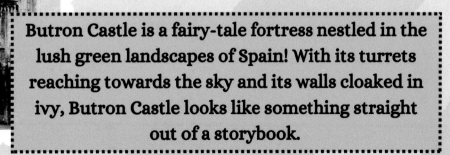

Butron Castle is a fairy-tale fortress nestled in the lush green landscapes of Spain! With its turrets reaching towards the sky and its walls cloaked in ivy, Butron Castle looks like something straight out of a storybook.

Meet the People

Spanish people, also known as "españoles", are known for their love of music, dance, and delicious food. They live in diverse regions across the country, from the sunny beaches of the coast to the picturesque villages in the mountains. Spanish people take great pride in their rich heritage and traditions, which are passed down from generation to generation. Flamenco dancing, bullfighting, and soccer (or "fútbol" as they call it) are popular hobbies that bring people together with laughter and excitement.

Spanish people also love to gather with family and friends to celebrate special occasions like festivals and fiestas, where they enjoy traditional foods, lively music, and colorful parades. From the vibrant streets of Madrid to the sunny shores of Barcelona, the people of Spain are known for their warmth, zest for life, and their love for fun and festivities!
Viva España!

¡Hola! Did you know that the official language of Spain is Spanish, or "Español" as they call it? It's a beautiful language with its own unique sounds and expressions that make it fun to learn! Spanish is spoken by millions of people all around the world, and it's the third most spoken language on the planet! In Spain, you'll hear people speaking Spanish with different accents and dialects depending on the region they're from, which makes it even more interesting and diverse.

Wildlife and Nature

¡Hola amigos! Welcome to the wild side of Spain! From soaring mountains to golden beaches, Spain is a land of diverse landscapes that are home to many fascinating animals. You might spot a majestic Iberian lynx roaming the forests, or catch a glimpse of a playful bottlenose dolphin leaping out of the sparkling Mediterranean Sea.

Spain is also famous for its brave bullfighters and their mighty bulls, who are admired for their strength and grace. But that's not all! Spanish people love their animals and take good care of them. You might see people walking their furry friends in the parks, or even taking their horses for a ride in the countryside.

Spain's warm climate and beautiful nature make it a perfect playground for all sorts of outdoor adventures, like hiking, birdwatching, and exploring the fascinating world of insects and butterflies. So get ready to embark on a wild journey through the breath-taking landscapes of Spain and discover its amazing wildlife! ¡Vamos a explorar! (Let's explore!)

Yummy Delights

¡Hola amigos! Are you hungry for some delicious Spanish delights? Spain is a food lover's paradise, with its rich culinary heritage and mouth-watering dishes that are loved by people all around the world. The national dish of Spain is the famous "paella," a scrumptious rice dish filled with juicy seafood, tender chicken, and flavourful vegetables. But that's just the beginning! Spain is also known for its tapas, which are small, tasty dishes that are perfect for sharing with friends and family. You can find tapas in almost every corner of Spain, from bustling markets to cosy little taverns. Some popular tapas include crispy patatas bravas, succulent chorizo, and savoury croquettes. Spanish people love to eat out, and you'll find plenty of amazing restaurants where you can indulge in mouth-watering Spanish cuisine.

So get ready to embark on a culinary adventure through the flavours of Spain and discover the joy of Spanish cuisine! ¡Buen provecho! (Bon appétit!)

SPANISH CUISINE

From fancy Michelin-starred restaurants to humble neighbourhood eateries, there's something for everyone. Spanish meals are often leisurely affairs, with families and friends coming together. Spanish people love to savour their meals, taking time to enjoy every bite and share stories around the table.

TORTILLA

PAELLA

CROQUETTES

Famous Figures

Spain is a land of incredible people who have left their mark in history, entertainment, and beyond. From brave explorers to talented artists, there are so many amazing personalities to learn about from Spain's rich heritage. You'll discover legendary historical figures like Christopher Columbus, who set sail on daring adventures to explore new lands and make incredible discoveries. Or Pablo Picasso, a world-renowned artist known for his unique and colorful masterpieces. Spanish royals like King Felipe VI and Queen Letizia, who represent their country with grace and elegance. And who can forget the iconic flamenco dancer, Carmen Amaya, whose graceful moves and passionate performances have captivated audiences around the world? There are also famous Spanish athletes like Rafael Nadal, a tennis superstar, and Sergio Ramos, a legendary football player.

So get ready to be inspired by the incredible people of Spain, who have made their mark on history and continue to shape the world with their talents and achievements! ¡Viva España!

Philip II of Spain was a notable historical figure who was known for his significant influence during the Spanish Golden Age

Born in 1491 in the Basque region of Spain, Ignatius Loyola initially pursued a military career, but his life took a dramatic turn after being seriously injured in battle. During his recovery, he experienced a profound spiritual awakening and dedicated his life to serving God

POPULAR FIGURES

Throughout history, Spain has been home to many famous figures who have left their mark on the world such as King Philip II of Spain, Salvador Dali and Ignatius Loyola.

In modern times, popular figures in Spain are often influenced by the media and other mediums, like movies, TV shows, and social media. Actors, musicians, and sports stars can become household names and inspire young people all around the world. It's important to remember that popularity can change over time, and there are many different ways that people can become famous and make a positive impact on society. So, whether it's through their talents, achievements, or contributions, Spanish figures throughout history have left an indelible mark on the world!

Miguel de Cervantes was a renowned Spanish writer and one of the most important figures in world literature.

Festivals and celebrations

Welcome to the colourful world of festivals and celebrations in Spain, where the joy and excitement never seem to end! Spain is known for its vibrant and lively festivities, with a rich tapestry of cultural traditions that are sure to captivate your imagination. From grand parades to music-filled street parties, Spain is a country that loves to celebrate! You'll be amazed by the dazzling costumes, rhythmic dances, and delicious treats that are part of Spain's rich tapestry of celebrations. Get ready to embark on a thrilling journey through the fiestas and festivals of Spain, where the spirit of celebration is alive and kicking all year round! Let's dive into the fascinating world of Spanish festivities and discover the magic that awaits!

THE MOST POPULAR RELIGIOUS HOLIDAY IN SPAIN IS CALLED SEMANA SANTA, WHICH MEANS "HOLY WEEK." IT'S A TIME WHEN THE WHOLE COUNTRY COMES ALIVE WITH MUSIC, COLOUR, AND POWERFUL TRADITIONS THAT HAVE BEEN PASSED DOWN THROUGH GENERATIONS. IMAGINE WALKING THROUGH THE STREETS AND SEEING HUGE PROCESSIONS OF PEOPLE WEARING ELABORATE ROBES AND CARRYING STATUES OF RELIGIOUS FIGURES, ALL WHILE THE AIR IS FILLED WITH THE SOUND OF DRUMS AND TRUMPETS. THE ATMOSPHERE IS ELECTRIC AS YOU WATCH THE "COFRADIAS," OR RELIGIOUS BROTHERHOODS, MARCHING WITH SOLEMNITY AND REVERENCE.

Daily Life

Welcome to the vibrant and lively daily life of the people of Spain! Here, work and play go hand-in-hand, and there's always something exciting happening. Spanish people are known for their strong work ethic and love for leisurely hobbies. They may work in bustling cities or quaint towns, and many enjoy taking a break in the afternoon for a siesta, a time to rest and recharge for the rest of the day.

Traveling is also a big part of Spanish culture, with many families taking trips to the beach, mountains, or historical landmarks during weekends and holidays. From the bustling streets of Madrid to the sunny beaches of Barcelona, Spain's daily life is full of energy, colour, and a zest for living that you're sure to love!

LIFE IN SPAIN

People in Spain have a vibrant and colorful sense of style that reflects their rich culture and traditions. You might spot them wearing bright and lively outfits, with traditional dresses like the "traje de flamenca" for women and the "traje corto" for men, especially during special celebrations and festivals. Spanish people love to interact with each other warmly and affectionately, with plenty of hugs, kisses, and friendly greetings. Family and friends are incredibly important in Spanish culture, and spending time together is cherished. When it comes to getting around, you'll often see Spaniards zipping around on scooters, bicycles, or even on foot, enjoying the sunny weather and lively streets. And if you're lucky, you might even catch a glimpse of a colorful flamenco dance performance, as dancing is a cherished art form in Spain. The Spanish way of life is filled with warmth, joy, and a love for their traditions and each other!

Fun Facts

Spain is a fascinating country with a rich history, diverse culture, and unique facts that make it special. Let's dive into some interesting facts about Spain!

1. Spain is famous for artists like Picasso and Dalí.
2. Spain has a special dance called flamenco with colorful costumes and footwork.
3. Spain has a tradition called "siesta," which is a nap after lunchtime.
4. Spain has famous soccer teams like FC Barcelona and Real Madrid.
5. Spain has a festival called "La Tomatina" where people throw tomatoes at each other!
6. Spain has ancient castles, palaces, and forts with knight and princess stories.
7. Spain has beautiful beaches for swimming and sandcastle building.

BEAUTIFUL SPAIN

Glossary

- Paella: A popular Spanish dish made with rice, meat, and seafood, often considered a national dish of Spain.
- Bullfighting: A traditional Spanish sport where people fight bulls in a large arena, though controversial in modern times.
- Gaudi: Antoni Gaudi, a famous architect from Spain known for his unique and colorful buildings, especially in Barcelona.
- Siesta: A traditional Spanish custom of taking a nap after lunchtime, especially in the warmer regions of Spain.
- Tapas: Small, delicious appetizers or snacks often served with drinks in Spain, a popular part of Spanish cuisine.
- Language: Spanish, also known as "español," is the official language of Spain and widely spoken throughout the country.

Made in United States
Orlando, FL
06 June 2025

61884917R00019